I Will Not Be A Butcher
For The Wealthy

T0312682

Anthony Seidman

I Will Not Be A Butcher For The Wealthy

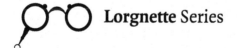 **Lorgnette** Series

First published in 2017
by Eyewear Publishing Ltd
Suite 333, 19-21 Crawford Street
Marylebone, London W1H 1PJ
United Kingdom

Typeset with graphic design by Edwin Smet
Author photo by Willivaldo Delgadillo
Printed in England by Lightning Source

ISBN 978-1-911335-82-5

Eyewear wishes to thank Jonathan Wonham for his generous patronage of our press.

WWW.EYEWEARPUBLISHING.COM

For Daniel, Leah and Nylsa

TABLE OF CONTENTS

SADDER THAN TRISTAN

Nobody has said the word *Mango* for days –
and it's enough to make me weigh two silver coins in one hand,
and a glass of ether in the other.
No one either has said *Azure*, *Mandolin*, or *Lagoon*;
plenty of *Autopsy*, plenty of *Vetting*,
or words nickel-tart like *Budget*, words that
bloat, like *Tariff*, words like feathers clumped in glue,
words more vacant than the eye of a tilapia
on a fish-monger's bed of ice;
words saccharine as *Blessing*, or blunted from
misuse like *Genius*, *Patriot*, or *Passion*.
No one has said the word *Mango* for ages,
let alone *Dune*, *Rose*, or *Dusk*;
no one has paused to simply utter *Word*,
like an appraiser peering into a diamond.
Already the uniforms are parading the *Crutches* before
the scurry of *Shrapnel* and *Lynching*
reaches the carbines, the warehouses hoarding
barrels of nightmare which clutter
the cold forest of rebar and stagnant water.

Some have agreed not to notice.

But I have heard the word *Earthquake*, the word *Carnage*,
a business suit sneezes when bats flap
from the pulpit in a *Cathedral* erected for manicures.
I haven't heard the word *Mango* for ages –
simple, round, and sweet. I haven't wept that fruition,
not yet, not for a while,
and that's what others mean when they say the word *Drought*.

A BODY ON FIRE IS ALWAYS IN NEED OF WATER

Some for slurring *mezcal*,
or hungering the black grip of leather;
some savoring the saliva stewing their tongues;
some, blue dentures spiked with diabetic fricassee;
some hear the glue drying, the paint peeling, their bones like wind
        blowing through
organ pipes when they snore atop roach cots;
some sweat while others jabber the psalms of molting spiders;
some, itching to swill turpentine;
some, itching with murder,
others, extortionists vomiting the tropics;
some drown in the darkness where light sneezes a tsunami;
some with long hearts, others disheartened, or shoveled coal,
but all twitch sleeplessness:
gazes threaded with blood-vessels more legible than cobwebs...
the Saints of Acne,
the Fedoras fearing rusted paperclips,
the Bomb-Makers allergic to chalk dust,
the Newly Pregnant and Already Miserable,
the Audited and the Shoe Sniffers wilting inside closets and elevators...
they all conjugate insomnia the way vodka distills the potato,
gelling like duck's shit atop a lake's surface,
latex gloves in a taxidermist's office,
always awake at the hour when blades nick,
the Signers of Contracts with Doctors of Debt,
the Slurpers of Chemical Gnosticism,
the Topographers of Bacterial Amnesia...
how I wish to embrace that river cluttered with mismatching shoes, busted dolls,
and pill-bottles,
not to mention scarves, toothpicks, aborted sonnets,
and scoop into my heart a catalog of mud,

to comb their hair,
weave black garlands round their thighs,
press my ear against their chest,
osculate their bleeding gums,
emit the blue ribbon of mercy from their shattering teeth,
and drag them inside,
find them some benches in this poem
gestated on a night when guitars and pistols blazed the thirst
of the Convulsive,
the Horrendous,
the split toenail on the Goat's left foot.

EMPATHY LACKS POSTAGE AND CAN'T BE E-MAILED AS AN ATTACHMENT

I thought no one listened,
but I heard about a letter which had yet to reach me.

Who was I?
Clay. Bone-marrow. Pin-point of ink.

I didn't think of myself as a hairdo,
a tie, longer than the Mississippi, and rhetoric against
rapscallions scooping free Prozac into cadaverous jaws.

If I could sniff the letter, such prescience
of parking fines, hang-overs, asbestos, rust.

I tremble like
jungle canopies before the boom of Napalm.

The letter I imagined: an answer,
like the engine locking, smoking, screeching,
after the oil has burned to pure heat.

But the letter doesn't flick into my hands.

Why do the clouds stutter?!

I await the letter which has yet to be written, signed
with a signature, as flowery as an Alabaman's evening greetings,
his cheeks red, his jowls jubilant, and a white
kerchief in his right fist, as he wipes sweat from brow.

I await the letter whose author
surely over-estimates me,
because he addressed me as Dear Sir,
and by the time the mail reaches my box,
Miss Evening,
whose gnarled fingers scratch at my bald pate,
making sure it glistens free
of pigeon shit, gnashed spiders.
She, who cackles phlegm,
that Spinster Aunt, will make certain
my forehead & scalp pave a highway where
the drivers will pass a shack by a yucca and chaparral field,
and by a moon-pale boy, his head
resting in his hands,
elbows resting on a window ledge.

The letter would contain the code to a safe containing Autumn's toxin in a vial.
The letter would dragonfly, stray-dog, jitterbug, and then spontaneous-combust.
The letter, lattice of sadness, acrid chocolate, & green vomit deemed as
            cough syrup.
The letter, no private cognac for the suit and tie, but universal sludge.
The letter, a transcript of telephone sex between monkey & shoe-horn.
The letter, the Map for the Minotaur, so he may – at last! –
escape from the labyrinth – shaped like a pile of filthy sneaker laces –
then pose for the cameras at The Threshold's opening while tipping a top hat.
The letter, a chair painted red,
empty, in the middle of a chamber 10,000 leagues beneath the sea.
The letter, combustive sugar.
The letter, cupola-styled architecture as a form of dysentery.
The letter, dictated in the language of tar, collision of asteroids, suicide by Disney,
blackboards cluttered with the algebra of moths, coupons for canned chili.
The letter, what's swept under the garage.
What simmers in the millionaire's private safe.
Gunpowder in a moll's mascara.

Machine-guns mistaken for lightning-rods,
when the tender marionettes of meat waltzed before their aim.

The letter would prove
a fitting cornerstone to shattered store windows,
beets boiled, stuffed with shit then fed to the Kittens of Holy Charity,
leather sandals dipped in goat's broth, and served to Bankers as an amuse-bouche,
while the owners of leather sandals sniff deposits of plastic jerky for nutrients,
and send money-grams charged with the energy
of owls perched on coffins, or strippers hooked
to antidepressants, or cheerleaders
licking the chilly urinals of high school distinction.

But no letter will reach me.

No arsenic blooms in my left eye. No
cactus asks the clouds why they pour vultures, no
mercurochrome for the sun's gash on its right cheek, no
boxing-gloves for a petal who once wielded a tequila bottle.

I can't swallow this without vomiting, –
not taxicabs, nor OxyContin, nor candles lit following the repast of chicken's fat
nor pure Mondays near the blue tongue of seagulls,
will pull me up through the toxins drifting above my parking lot,
those zeppelins of brownness woven thick as sweaters for the Dakotas.

Give me the grace,
O Expanse of Dark Matter & Isolate Flecks of Helium,
to be no more a martyr than the mountain lion
rifled for encroaching upon a Millionaire's estate in the hills,
or the arrow-riddled Saint whose
agile body writhed in the shape of sensuous flames
as he sank, blood-glazed and
basted with agony,
down the Mastiff Pole of Punishment.

DEER ARE NEXT ON THE LIST

Starting at Alpha, thunder thrusts a claw across the horizon, then reaches Omega,
which is here, in an open fist, a marble still moist and scooped
from the gaping left-eye-socket of an old man who
escaped the home, wanders the rain, naked,
on a boulevard of smokestacks and motels, meandering;
a marble that once rolled over dirt in a playground
where boys caught beetles green as cough lozenges,
ripped off their wings, and sneezed soda-caps.
It's a little heaven and earth pent-up inside, smaller
than the asphalt tundra now enveloping the globe,
and therefore more asphodel, more verdurous.
Although swaths of cumulus drift within this blink of blue,
the henchmen weighed down by ingots
point, gesticulate at the gutted mountain
and insist "The verb must feed on vanished silver!"

So. If you weep at 5 o'clock in the desert,
(not too far from here, and vast as Tanguy),
nothing will blossom, and as always
the Gila monster will marinate in his venom;
but closer to the sea, on an esplanade unmarred by tar,
some Beauty called Unreality will turn
and face every nerve yearning for siesta, twilight, hearth.
And the portal teetering on the beginning & the end
will bloom backwards into protozoa.

That's what can't be put into words, let alone music.

ONLY THE GREAT, ONLY THE AUGMENTED

Far down the winter wood
the gown of the last
castrato
rustles in the wind.
He shivers
having waited there
since daybreak, lips parted, ear
and head bent towards
the clack of ice-sheets dislodging
from pines and
shattering on the frozen floor.
No other accompaniment
reaches him, no
other pitch, there, in the woods
except for the ice and
the bleating
of his forced baritone.

I WON'T DISGUISE MYSELF AS A STEAKHOUSE FOR THE WEALTHY

Now's the ascension of the Orange Monkey.
Deodorize my ears as he stammers from the Boughs of the Gold-Plated,
and let the Impressionist Tableaux sweating in Los Angeles museums
ooze purple & blue toadstools beneath the oven-sun;
let the clouds yawn, then snoop back into a squint of drought like
a self-puckering asshole seeking the company of polyps.

Enough months of linen and lemons as weighty as a bull's testicles;
I was spoon-fed a granularity of cardboard and sugar
which militaries use as housing for hurricane victims,
or as hair-dye for a Slavic distension whose breasts
have ballooned memes slathered with mayonnaise.

Now's the ascension of the Orange Monkey,
and Ariadne's running amok, gleeful,
in her labyrinth on the sunny side of delirium.

I despise the fruit dangling from the Orange Monkey's lowest branches,
as luscious as bacteria basting a freshly used latex glove.

Perfume-pump the few words not yet chained,
and let them rise above the topmost branches
before hornets zip them into bits of confetti.
But no one will be collecting the shards of color.
No one – soon – will waltz without a mask.

Mace and a mainlined dosage of TNT won't cure you of necrotic newsreels.

Some say the statues of saints have stung doorbells,
asking for a place to stay,
and if they can crash on the couch.

I try to stay in shape, on my mark,
ready to go.

I explode the host of leather methane-gas-bags;
I tight-rope-walk the eyebrows of crooked stock-charts;
I glue arsenic to the teeth of newspapers kissing mendacities;
but I fail when it comes to a sudden splendor of butterfly,
when remembering why my youth rattles a boxcar across fields below zero,
and I fail when listening to the better wisdom
of a chained dog howling in a warehouse.

Ah! There are some tomorrows too distant,
like sunlight on a bather's hips, She
who turns the rum galleons back on their heels,
some tomorrows where everything breaks beforehand,
because the Jackals want you to dress up as a waiter
for surgery on broken hearts,
because many clamor for a steakhouse above the slums,
(with a neon sign made of polysynthetic flutes & smiling tumors.)

Don't be fooled by that skyscraper.
It's the Tree of Stoopid,
the Tree of coiffures that code one milkshake for a thousand Bolivian hens,
the Tree of titanium tirades, small orgasms injected into mouthfuls of heartburn,
the Tree with roots that snag 1,000 miles below the ocean's surface,
only to surface and
froth pesticides into the breast-milk of Icelandic mothers.

Oh the Monkey, he's Orange, Golden,
like microwaved cough-syrup gooped on canapés of Mandarin nightmare.
Take care, the Dakota fields they combust,
take care, the Antillean isles ache
in their loins like an adolescent kicked to the strip-club's curb;
take cover the African lion, the domesticated zebra, and the coal of Pennsylvania;
there are gasmasks giftwrapped for you,

projectiles that vibrate and bing at you,
hallways longer than midnight,
painted white,
and that won't dry their interrogation light
until the Tree of Stoopid blazes, carbonizes, and falls.

What astounds me...
is how the crumple of cry in the lily,
the mitochondria's steam-engine-chugging & tenacity,
not to mention the seasons' rusty wheels,
or the burst of blue-whale over surface
then his plunge as his baleen sieve steals
8,000 lbs. of krill,
how all of that
may continue.

This fragile glass of the world wilts me,
while I knuckle a turnip to bloody.

LAST RANT BEFORE I'M DENIED ENTRY INTO MY BIG TOE

The napalms are sprouting palm trees.

The beheadings are spitting roses.

The vertical, steel planks open deserts.

But I am the forgotten being;
forgotten, the thin lips sealed against the gathering asbestos;
forgotten, the computer chip in my molar, the hair-long sperm slivering its tail
    beneath the photo on my passport, and my plasma as valuable as cheeseburger;
forgotten, for sipping sin, but no gold, for desiring the bride's tears, but no
    Minotaur;
forgotten, with a suitcase of dirt and tooth-brush;
forgotten for believing in a marble column;
forgotten, but dreaming slow descent into a dome of blue, vapor-trails weaving
    their psalms praising potable soda-pop, and cellphones for espionaged teeth;
forgotten, like the dimwit seated on the curb outside a charred orphanage and
    slurping rattlesnacks from a paper bag.

My sleep has been the cinder-block hut,
now a tetanus nest of rebar;
my good morning,
bells clanging to ears looped along a jailer's key-ring;
my bride,
a red dress snapping in the wind & snagged on the claws of an acacia tree;
my morning commute to work, some minaret belching carbon or
assembly line inserted inside the burro spray-painted with zebra stripes;
my beer & repast of salt,
shavings of cardboard;
my daughter,
a plastic tiara, a soiled pink dress, a roller-skate, wheels still spinning in a landfill;
my ecstasy,
a stray mutt mounting a poodle in an alley with malarial puddles;

my absolution,
water's squirt, squeegee, and rag I use to cleanse your windshield.

So.

Is this the decline and fall?
Is this the partition carved from unused antidepressants where children kick
    a soccer ball?
Is this a corner where I tremble while coyotes and possums repossess the
    brittle chassis of my biography?
Is this the kind cultural anthropologist who will listen to my astrology
    of implosions?
Is this the eviction from the carousel inside a suburban mall?
Is this the thread thru the labyrinth into a kitchen where I assemble
    kale & raw tuna?

No, no.

The palm-trees are sprouting napalm.

The roses are blooming beheadings.

The deserts are slapping new paint on a wall.

This is the charnel house primeval;
this is the loving-kindness medieval;
this is the suit stuffed with processed meat, cow-lungs, pig-hearts, and
rhetoric burping judges who pledge allegiance to the crow.

This is the crumpling teeth who wish to intone spirituals but lack courage.
This is the fork in one fist, and snake in the other.
This is the promise for homeland, as long as it's under water.
This is the story of smolder,
a fire without flames.

This is a shrimp cocktail in a steakhouse for the wealthy.

MORE CORROSIVE THAN CLOUDS

What an exquisite perfume is grief.

Wave your *mouchoir*!

Ants, flies crowd that sweat.

Lemon, butyric acid, cognac, a faint
pellet of turd, strawberry, the peppery waft from axilla

compose it.

Not to mention blood,
diesel fumes from tail-pipe,
or the crisp sheet of morning news.

The Absurd is revealed when one takes a whiff!

Denuded, one can glance at the moon
and register the topsy-turvy climate: hellish & arctic.
Not the argent field reserved for reverie.

Life becomes a map as etiolated
as the bones of fried tilapia picked clean.

And you exhale.

And all of a sudden it's as if clouds were made of stone,
or when touching the flesh of your child or mate,
you tune the bone, and not the nerves.

Then everyone, your dawdling grandparent,

attendant at the corner store, driver
idling at the red light in a sedan sleeker than yours...
objects for the skull-rack.

And to think some constituents question the validity
of a free meal for a darker child, or how words in a foreign tongue
sit ox-heavy on a tongue preferring tennis.

Yes, Callimachus, no delight like a few trochees, unmixed
wine blacker than the black earth,
and passing out.

SUNDAYS ARE RESERVED FOR SUICIDE

Let not the sun dip her fingers in a Fedora and opt for the sweat of an
       accountant as soul-salve.
Let not the pain in a man's chest fade until he weeps the incinerated
       home of a desert family.
Let not the lamentations fade until the boxcars cease rattling, open, and
       release magnetized smoke.
Let us not weep until the paint dries (and never will it).
Let us not weep until the stone opens, revealing her yolk.
Let us not weep until guitars brood black and pianos flutter like bats.
Let us not cut our thick tresses with shears because of hexameters, wine, Demon.
Let us not weep.
Let not the Ghost of a Flea spit viral into your fitful sleep.
Let not sugar dissolve only to reveal the skull of an extinct saurian.
Let not virginity be confused with beer swilled from a daisy.
Instead
let us bake work boots,
let us twist rattlesnakes into the tableaus of the perpetually bored,
let us torment the black glove
then marvel at the butterfly molesting the pollen.
Perhaps Mondays will ripple the blue tapestry of a poem!
Over the honeycomb of an adolescent boy alone in a bathroom stall,
over the pleasures of razor,
the swift flight of soaring past the radiation of Jupiter while
a million men click their password or asphyxiate prisoners with plastic bags,
over ambivalent masochism,
over the smoking fields once jungles, and the nervous
twitching of ants as they map a trail towards annihilation,
over it all, including blade, bottle, hydrogen, and Key,
perhaps there may still flutter
the ragged black & blue flag of Ecstasy.

LOOSEN MY LIPS

When I can't speak, spider-fangs
pierce my gums, numbing them so that
my saliva pours freely, my jaw slackens,
and the spider spins ink,
and the ink spits a web of babble;
I sit in the corner where the forlorn boy
stockpiles his blades, matches, dolls,
and journal hoarding a sentence that runs for 200 pages,
not including several diluvials: thinning hair,
a mortgage, anxiety trapped within a briefcase.

When I can't listen, a mosquito circles my left ear,
a whisper from a crack in the floor-boards
rises to my right ear, and I sweat the gust from an opened door,
the moon vibrates the climate of
overturned sedans, bonfires at intersections, bullets,
and the lights, one by one, click off,
boulevards plunge into sudden midnight,
cars stop running, windows lock,
storefronts and hearths shut down because
the scream inside my skull echoes continents.

When I can't taste, my tongue has been napping with the worms;
the soil crumbles corn husks left in the vacant lot of August,
or fingers of a grandmother weaving the silken tresses of her granddaughter;
I smile and remember the lemons, so blinding,
and the time I bit into one, unpeeled, direct from bough, and winced.

When I can't smell, postcards damp with the humidity
of ports where men sweat as sailors or money-lenders, and women brood,
reach my mailbox, and the spidery script of a fountain pen

prescribes treatments for a ripe olfactory: hot tar,
scent of a seamstress's hair after 12 hours of work, gas fumes, chalk dust.

When I can't see, I know the fools have set me
on a golden throne, and my feet, shod with velvet slippers.
Elsewhere: peasant girls, raped. Towers burning.

When I can't dream, the scripture in a clay tablet
buried beneath a millennia of floods, sand-storms, and bloody altars,
shifts my wisdom teeth so that I can chew on termites drilling the wood
       of sleep.

When I can't touch, I am the wind.

SO THAT NIGHT SHORTEN ITS HOURS

I avoid stairs zigzagging towards basements
flooded with formaldehyde, and
leaving their residue in the strawberry
I savor, or the glass of mineral water.
I conceal my concerns,
I erase chalked quotients from the blackboard,
I commit a smile.

I find myself, landed gentry,
enthroned on a patch of stucco and electricity.
But wasn't I once the footsteps
entering the tunnel, the angular chin
bent on eviscerating the bull,
my xiphos
steaming with fresh blood,
wiped to a glisten against a wool cloak?

Or am I the farce of that fantastical scrap
sticking to my finger like a wasp?

Each day, the sun, a spider in the palm trees,
the agony of dogs,
the caravan of merchants revving their Jeeps,
the bus benches like saddles buckled around bellies of smog,
the hammers, the medicinal sandwiches, the liquor,
the orchards, the blood-banks,
the matrons snoring in their blue chambers,
the roads rumored to smack into prosperity,
is it all the real, the
Honest-to-God Drachma?

I conceal my concerns,
I commit a smile.

Far off, there's a vendor selling jugs of night,
and they weigh no more than a jar of honey,
and he sells them even after dusk, when there's no light.

And his shelves turn so dark in the darkness,
and the surrounding darkness turns darker yet...
but there are some lights on, some taverns stirring,
and I am neither comforted, nor thirsty...
and I don't know if I should smile, or place a bet.

ACKNOWLEDGEMENTS

My deepest gratitude to Todd Swift and others at Eyewear Publishing for their dedication to poetry, and for taking on this unruly suite of poems. My thanks especially to Rosanna Hildyard for honing this pamphlet. Additional thanks to Paul Roth for always supporting my work, as well as for publishing a significant amount of poems included here within *The Bitter Oleander*, and to Alan Britt and Patrick Lawler for their endorsements.

Some poems have previously been published in *Alligator Zine*, *Caliban* and *The Bitter Oleander*.

Lightning Source UK Ltd.
Milton Keynes UK
UKOW04f0008200717
305649UK00001B/13/P